THE LITTLE WITCH'S CHRISTMAS BOOK

by Linda Glovach

Prentice-Hall, Inc., Englewood Cliffs, N.J.

10 9 8 7 6 5 4 3 2

Printed in the United States of America • J

Prentice-Hall International, Inc., London
Prentice-Hall of Australia, Pty. Ltd., North Sydney
Prentice-Hall of Canada, Ltd., Toronto
Prentice-Hall of India Private Ltd., New Delhi
Prentice-Hall of Japan, Inc., Tokyo

Library of Congress Cataloging in Publication
Data

Glovach, Linda.
    The little witch's Christmas book.

    SUMMARY: The little witch demonstrates
how she celebrates a traditional Christmas with
her family and friends. Includes instructions for
making invitations, presents, and decorations.
    1. Christmas—Juvenile literature. 2. Christ-
mas decorations—Juvenile literature. [1. Christmas. 2. Christmas decorations] I. Title.
TT900.C4G54   745.5   74-2371
ISBN 0-13-537951-2

TABLE OF CONTENTS

THE LITTLE WITCH'S CODE

1. The little witch gives herself plenty of time to make all her cards and packages so she can deliver something to everyone on her list in time for Christmas.

2. The little witch helps set the table for her mother and straighten the house for her father because she knows her parents are especially busy at holiday time.

3. The little witch knows everyone likes to be remembered at Christmas time. She makes stockings and other surprises for people who can't look forward to Christmas with their families.

4. Whether she's making taffy or trimming the tree, the little witch puts safety first at Christmas time. She never uses the stove without her mother's help. And around the tree she is careful not to touch the electric lights or decorate branches that are out of easy reach.

I. GETTING READY FOR CHRISTMAS

GOING SHOPPING

The very first thing the little witch does to get ready for Christmas is to make a shopping list. She writes down all the things she will need to make her cards, presents and decorations.

The little witch makes her own Christmas cards and presents early and delivers them in her Santa sack.

CHRISTMAS SHOPPING LIST
by LITTLE WITCH

CONSTRUCTION Paper
Tempera Paints
marking Pens
glitter
Crayons
glue
STRING
Clear TAPE
Green Kraft Paper

Cranberries
POPcorn
Holly
COTTON
Small wrapped CANDY
Candy canes
Wrapping Paper
Ribbon
mistletoe

MAKING CARDS

SPOOKY CHRISTMAS GHOST

You need: green construction paper, 10" x 19"; white and red tempera paint; ruler; pencil; scissors; marker pen.

Fold the length of the paper in half. Measure 1¾" in from each side and mark two dots on top fold. From the dots draw the ghost, as shown in the picture. Cut out ghost but do not cut between the dots on the fold. Cut eyeholes only in front piece, not in back piece. Paint front of ghost white. Paint *scary* and *Christmas* in the eyeholes in red. Open the card and paint *Merry* next to *scary*. Write receiver's name and sign your name on card.

FAMILY FACES CHRISTMAS CARD

You need: 2 pieces of shirt cardboard, each 12" x 16"; photographs of each person in your family; pencil; ruler; scissors; crayons; glue.

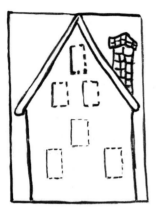

Draw a house on one sheet of cardboard. Include a window for each member of your family.

Cut along the dotted lines of each window, as shown in the picture. Do not cut along the solid lines.

After you have cut out each window, draw a pencil line around each one on the second piece of cardboard, as shown in the picture.

Paste the photographs in the areas marked on the second piece of cardboard.

Place the cardboard with your drawing of the house on top of the cardboard with the photographs.

Glue the 2 pieces of cardboard together at all 4 corners. Color in the house. The little witch also makes a door, which she cuts on 3 sides, as shown in the picture.

She writes a message under the door.

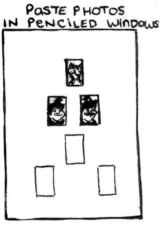

PASTE PHOTOS
IN PENCILED WINDOWS

GLUE PIECES OF
CARDBOARD TOGETHER.

DRAW DOOR.
CUT ON DOTS ONLY
WRITE CHRISTMAS MESSAGE ON DOOR

SURPRISE STOCKING CARD

You need: 2 pieces of red construction paper, 3″ x 6″; cotton; paints; pencil; scissors; clear tape; glue.

Draw a stocking shape on one piece of paper and cut out. Trace stocking on the other piece of paper and cut out. Tape the two pieces together around sides and bottom.

Glue cotton around top rim. Write receiver's name and your name on front. Fill the stocking with candy canes or wrapped hard candies.

11

MAKING PRESENTS

ANIMAL MATCHBOX NECKLACE OR PILLBOX

You need: small matchbox; tempera paints; tiny piece of construction paper; scissors; glue; piece of string 20" long.

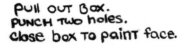

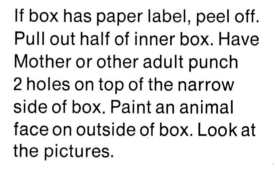

If box has paper label, peel off. Pull out half of inner box. Have Mother or other adult punch 2 holes on top of the narrow side of box. Paint an animal face on outside of box. Look at the pictures.

Make a snowy owl, a rabbit, a black cat.

Cut ears out of construction paper and glue them to back of box.

Draw the string through the holes (put a "lucky" penny inside if you like).
Do not attach string if you want to give as a pillbox.

BOOKMARK FUNNIES

You need: scissors; glue; a shirt cardboard; red felt; glitter.

Cut 2 or 3 of your friends' favorite cartoon characters out of newspaper or comic book.
Glue the characters onto a piece of shirt cardboard and cut them out.
Cut the shape of a Christmas stocking out of a piece of red felt.
Cut slits in the top of the stocking just wide enough to slip each of the comic characters through.
Put each character through a slot so that only the head shows.
Use glue with pointed spout. Squeeze gently as you write *Merry Christmas* across the bottom of the sock.
Sprinkle glitter over the glue and let dry.
Characters can be pulled out of the sock whenever a bookmark is needed.

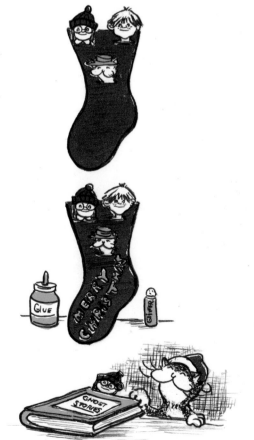

SANTA'S CANDY FACTORY

You need: ½ pint cream container; red construction paper, 3 pieces each 2¾″ x 2″ and 1 piece 1″ x ½″; 1 piece of brown paper, 1″ x 1½″; cotton; marker pen ; tempera paints; scissors; glue; small, wrapped hard candies.

Glue a piece of red paper to each side of carton. Let dry. Outline a 1″ x 1½″ door in front. Cut it out on top, right side and bottom. Do not cut on the left line. Glue the brown paper on the door.

Draw windows in the front and on the sides with marker pen.

Draw bricks over entire back and halfway up front and sides. Apply glue thickly on all sides of roof and paste cotton down to cover as snow.

Draw bricks on the chimney and glue to roof, as shown in picture.

CHRISTMAS CHIMNEY BANK

You need: empty cigar box; red construction paper; clear tape; scissors; black marker pen; black paint; cotton; glue.

Ask for an empty cigar box at the drugstore or stationery store. Have your mother or father help you cut a slot 2″ x ½″ at one end of the box.
Close the lid shut with clear tape.

Cut out pieces of red construction paper and glue them around the entire box. Be sure not to cover over the edges of the lid where it opens, so you can open the bank.

Draw a brick pattern on the paper with black marker.
Then paint the top of the chimney black and glue cotton around edges for snow.

WRAPPING PRESENTS

Cut off a sheet of wrapping paper large enough to cover all sides of your present. Bring one side of the paper about halfway over the box and tape it to the box. Bring the other side over that, and tape it down. Fold the paper down over the side. Fold corner ends in, into triangle shapes.

Bend triangle up onto the package and tape down. Do the same at the other end of the box.

GIFT TAGS

Make your gift tags out of colored construction paper, 1″ x 3″. Punch a hole at one end of the tag and put a string through it. Tape to your present.

BOWS

You need: ribbon; scissors; clear tape.

Cut off a 48″ strip of ribbon and loop it around your fingers 8 or 10 times. The wider apart you hold your fingers the bigger the bow will be. Hold the ribbon pinched together in the middle and cut a groove on each edge.
Cut a strip of ribbon down the middle and tie it firmly around the grooves.

CUT GROOVES

Now pull out all the loops, and you have a fantastic bow.

Cut off a 24″ strip of ribbon. Wrap one end firmly around index and middle fingers. Continue wrapping more loosely with each circle. By wrapping the ribbon tightly or loosely you can get different results.

MAKING PARTY INVITATIONS

You need: green construction paper, 5″ x 7″; several colors of paints or crayons; pencil; ruler; scissors.

Fold the length of the paper in half.

With the fold on the left, draw a jagged line like stair steps from the top left corner of the paper to 1″ from the bottom right corner.

Draw a straight line from the bottom of the jagged line across to ½″ from fold of the paper. From there draw a straight line to the bottom of the paper.

Cut along the lines you have drawn.

Write your guest's name on the outside of the card. Open the card and write the time, date and place of your party.

Then draw or paint decorations on your Christmas tree invitation.

II. CHRISTMAS PARTIES

TAFFY PULL

The little witch invites her friends over to share in the gooey fun of a taffy pull. Each one brings food coloring in a color he likes, or a small bottle of flavoring to make the taffy his favorite flavor.

You need: 1½ cups sugar
½ cup light corn syrup
¼ cup water
2 tablespoons butter
⅛ teaspoon salt
½ teaspoon vanilla extract

Put all ingredients except extract in a saucepan. Cook to about 270 degrees Fahrenheit (soft crack stage). Do not stir candy while cooking. Pour onto buttered platter.
As candy cools, lift edges toward center. When cool enough to handle, add extract and coloring. Butter fingertips, pull and stretch taffy in long ropes until it is light. Then cut into pieces with scissors while it is soft. Wrap the taffy you don't eat in plastic wrap and put in a container, or save for Santa Claus.

CAROLING PARTY

The little witch and her friends dress in their warmest clothes and go caroling around the neighborhood. Before leaving home, they practice their Christmas songs and then plan their singing route. Each member of the group takes turns carrying the flashlight and leading the way.

When they get home, everyone warms up with hot chocolate around a crackling fire.

PIÑATA PARTY

One of the little witch's favorite pastimes is a ghost piñata party. She fills the piñata with candy wrapped in brightly colored waterproof paper. The little witch and her mother also include inexpensive, unbreakable toys, which they wrap in aluminum foil. Since they need lots of room for their piñata game, the little witch and her friends go outdoors and gather around a tree. Everyone dresses warmly and wears boots because sometimes it takes a while to break the piñata.

You need: white tissue paper; a large grocery bag; wrapped candies; 8' piece of string; scissors; glue; pencil; construction paper.

Fill the bag with candy and tie top with string.

Cut the tissue paper into 5" wide strips and long enough to go around the grocery bag.

Fold each strip in half lengthwise.

Cut 1" into the folded edge, at ½" intervals.

Fold strips back at crease and glue halves together. This will makes loops fluff out. Glue strips around sack until it is covered.

Cut out features from construction paper and paste in place on the piñata.

Glue a large sheet of tissue paper around the bottom of the sack to make the ghost's body.

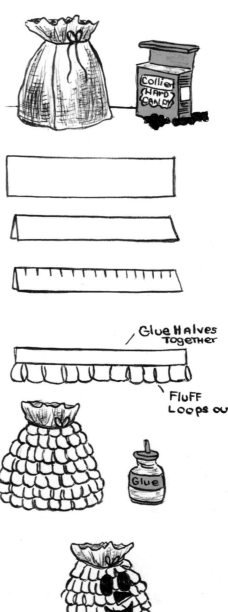

Glue Halves Together

Fluff Loops Out

Now you're ready to play the game the little witch plays with her ghost piñata. The little witch's father puts the string over a branch of the tree and holds on to the string. Each guest is given three chances to swing a bat at the ghost and break it open. Her father tugs on the string when he thinks the player will swing, making it harder to win. The first player to break open the ghost piñata wins, but everyone shares the candy.

BEAN KING AND QUEEN PARTY

During the twelve days there are many festivities and friendship gatherings. The little witch holds a Bean King and Queen party. She bakes a cake in which she has hidden a bean. When her friends arrive, they sit around the table, and the whole cake is cut into even pieces, one slice for each person.

If a boy finds the bean in his slice, he is King and chooses a Queen. If a girl finds the bean, she is Queen and picks a King. The couple then put on their crowns and sit next to each other. They will have good luck all year.

CROWNS (make 2)

You need: a strip of yellow construction paper or white paper painted gold, 3″ x 24″; pencil; scissors; stapler; paints.

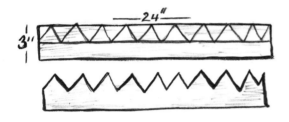

Draw a pencil line along the center of the length of the strip. Draw crown points from the line to the edge of the paper, each point about 1½″ apart. Cut out.

Paint jewels and designs on the crown. Overlap the ends to fit your head size and staple closed.

BEAN KING AND QUEEN CAKE

Set oven at 350 degrees. Mix ¼ cup of **margarine** and 1 cup of **sugar.** Sift together 2 cups of **flour**, 2 tablespoons of **baking powder** and one teaspoon of **salt.**
Mix the flour mixture, a half cup at a time, with the margarine and sugar mixture, alternating with 1¾ cup **milk.** Stir until the mixture is smooth and creamy. Add a **dried kidney bean** and stir until it is hidden. Pour into a greased, lightly floured loaf pan. Bake for 35 minutes. Cool the cake for at least an hour.

While you are waiting, make...

SNOWY FROSTING

Mix one cup of confectionery sugar with ¼ cup of soft butter. Stir together with a wooden spoon. Then add 1 tablespoon of milk, 1 teaspoon of vanilla and a teaspoon of salt.

Mix until the frosting is creamy at the low speed of your mixer. Spread over the cooled cake with a spatula.

III. CHRISTMAS AT HOME

MAKING A GINGERBREAD HOUSE

On the eighth day of Christmas the little witch makes a gingerbread house. She asks Mother and a friend to help her. It's fun to make and not too hard. The hard part is waiting until after Christmas to eat it.
The house is made out of four large cookies. Everything is good to eat except the roof and base, which are cardboard. This recipe makes a crisp, brittle cookie.

SANTA'S GINGERBREAD HOUSE

Sift together 5 cups sifted all purpose **flour**, 1 teaspoon **soda**, and 3 teaspoons **ginger**. Melt 1 cup **shortening** in saucepan large enough for mixing dough. Add 1 cup **sugar** and 1 cup **molasses.** Mix with hand until dough forms a ball. Put dough on a tabletop or board. Knead with your hands until it is easy to work with.

Flour the board lightly and roll out dough with rolling pin to ⅛″ thickness.

Cut out four walls according to the measurements shown. Cut a 1″ x 2″ door and a 1″ x 1″ window out of one wall. Do not lose the door.

Cut ½″ x 1″ shutters out of remaining dough. Cut small round cookies, little Christmas trees (you can ice them green) and gingerbread elves. Place dough on lightly greased cookie sheet. Bake at 325 degrees for about 15 minutes. Remove from sheet immediately and let cool.

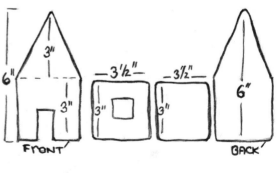

33

ROOF AND BASE

Cut 2 pieces of cardboard each 6½″ x 4″ for roof and 1 piece 4″ x 3″ for base. Wrap cardboards in white dinner napkins as snow and tape down.

To form roof put the two pieces side by side. Fasten together with clear tape. Bend to form roof.

Mix 1 cup confectionery sugar with 2 tablespoons of water to make a thick icing to hold walls together.

Stand the walls on the cardboard base on a white plate. Hold them up temporarily with small boxes. Attach walls together with thick strips of icing at all four corners and on top rim of cookies. Set the roof on. Let house dry thoroughly.

The chimney is a large red gumdrop with dab of icing for smoke. Paste Santa's house sign on roof. Large marshmallows make stools. A candy cane with address written on paper and glued on is the signpost.

ICING FOR WALLS

Mix 1½ cups confectionery **sugar** with 4½ table-spoons of **water** until icing is smooth, and spread on walls with a knife. Quickly decorate walls with **cookies, candy corn,** and **gumdrops.** Cover the door and shutters with **red hots.** Let dry thoroughly.

MAKING A WREATH

The little witch makes her own Christmas wreath to hang on her front door.

You need: a coathanger; 14 pieces of bendable wire, each 4″ long; Christmas tree clippings; holly sprigs; red satin ribbon.

Have your father take apart a coathanger and reshape it into a circle.

Twist one end around the other so the circle won't come apart.

Place a tree clipping lengthwise on the coathanger.

Wrap a piece of wire around both the clipping and the coathanger.

Put the next clipping on the circle slightly overlapping the first.

Continue this way until you have covered the whole coathanger.

Place a few holly sprigs around your wreath in the same way that you attached the tree clippings.

TYING A BOW

Make a loop with the ribbon.
Wrap the left side of the ribbon around once.

Make another loop and pull it
through the opening, as
shown.

Pull on both loops to tighten
the knot.

On each side of the knot tie a
piece of red thread and attach
the bow to the wreath.

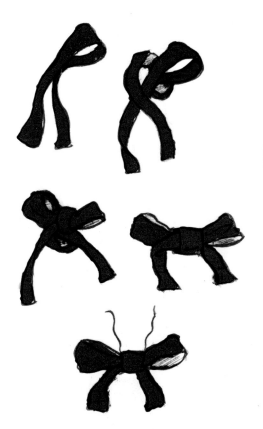

DECORATING THE HOUSE

The little witch loves to decorate her house with mistle-toe, holly and a special wreath she makes herself.

She and her father tape mistletoe above every doorway. She knows she'll get a Christmas smooch if someone catches her beneath it.

To decorate her mantle, she places holly leaves around candlesticks and burns bayberry candles.
For a centerpiece decoration, the little witch makes a holly tree. You need: an empty margarine container; holly leaves; a few Christmas tree clippings.
Punch holes in the lid and put holly stems through the holes.
Put tree clippings around the container.

DECORATING THE TREE

On Christmas eve the little witch goes with her family to buy a Christmas tree. Then they take it home and decorate it.

STRINGING POPCORN

The little witch decorates her tree with strands of popcorn. She invites her friends over and gives each guest a sewing needle threaded with a 4′ strand of thread (her mother does the threading).

Put the needle through each kernel of popcorn, near the brown center but not through it. *Always* keep your fingers clear of the needle point. Pull the first popcorn kernel all the way down to the knot. Pull each threaded kernel down next to the one before it. Hang the popcorn strands over the tree branches.

You can also string fresh cranberries. Be sure to do this right after you buy them when the berries are firm.

Put the needle through the longest part of the cranberry, pull the berry down to the knot and continue as with stringing popcorn.
For variety, you can put cranberries and popcorn on the same strand of thread.

WISE MEN'S CROWNS

You need: a toilet-paper cardboard cylinder, cut in 1″ cross sections; gold paint; ruler; pencil; scissors; tempera.

Measure ½″ down from top. Draw a line around ring. From line to top of ring make crown points. Cut out on the points. Paint the crowns gold, and decorate. Slip over a tree branch.

LITTLE WITCH'S HATS

Make 10 hats, most of them black but a few red and some green ones too.

For each hat you need: construction paper, one piece a half of a 6″ diameter circle and one piece a 3″ diameter circle; stapler; clear tape; pencil; scissors.

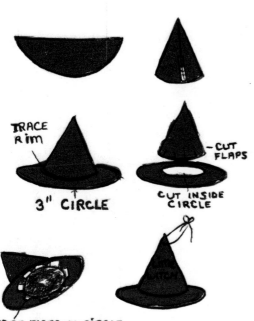

TRACE RIM

3″ CIRCLE

CUT INSIDE CIRCLE

CUT FLAPS

TAPE FLAPS TO CIRCLE

Roll the half circle into a cone. Staple and tape closed. Trace rim of cone in center of circle. Cut out inside the circle so it is smaller than cone rim. Cut ¼″ slits ½″ apart along rim of cone. Bend as flaps.

Slip circle down over cone and tape flaps to circle. Have Mother punch two tiny holes on each side of cone point. Put string through the holes and tie the hats on the tree. Each member in the family can paint his name on a hat.

FRIENDSHIP CHRISTMAS TREE

The little witch makes a friendship Christmas tree. She fills it with "bulbs" and hangs it on the inside of her front door. She keeps crayons and marker pens nearby and asks each visitor who comes to her house to sign his or her name on one of the bulbs and make a little design on it. When the tree is filled, she puts it in her front window and starts a new tree on her door.

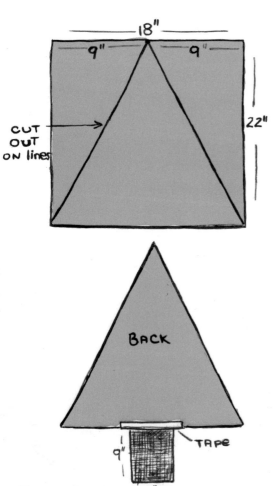

You need: 1 piece of green kraft paper, 18″ x 22″, or paint a white piece green; 1 piece, 6″ x 9″, painted brown; assorted colors of construction paper; pencil; ruler; colored marker pens; crayons; rubber cement; scissors; tape.

Mark a dot 9″ from either side of the green paper at the top of the 18″ side. Draw diagonal lines from the dot to each corner. Cut out on lines. Tape the 6″ side of brown paper to the bottom of cone as a tree trunk. Turn tree around so tape is in back. Put a strip of tape over opening line in front.

Cut bulbs out of construction paper. Use rim of water glass for size. Make some bells and triangles too. Glue bulbs and other ornaments to tree.
Cut a yellow star out of construction paper, write your name on it and glue it to top of tree.

Keep the crayons and marker pens nearby and ask each visitor to sign a bulb and draw a pretty design on it.

TWELFTH NIGHT

On the Twelfth Night, the eve of January 6, the final and
biggest celebration occurs.
The neighbors on the little witch's block put their
Christmas trees together in a pile and burn them in one
tremendous bonfire. They sing Christmas carols and ex-
change greetings.
Later everyone goes home for a big dinner to celebrate
the coming of the wise men with gifts for the newborn
Christ Child.

INDEX